Depression Workbook
70 Self-help techniques for recovering from depression

Tim Watkins
for
Life Surfing

ISBN-13: 978-1492719595
ISBN-10: 1492719595

CONTENTS

ABOUT THE AUTHOR

Tim Watkins is a Wellbeing Coach, Trainer and founder-director of Life Surfing, a not-for-profit company established to help prevent mental illness and to promote wellbeing.

Tim Watkins graduated from the University of Wales College Cardiff with a first class honours degree in 1990.

Between 1990 and 1997 he worked as a research officer for the Welsh Consumer Council where he researched and wrote a range of reports including *In Deep Water* an investigation into problems in the aftermath of the North Wales ("Towyn") floods of 1990, and *Quality of Life and Quality of Service* an investigation into the promotion of quality of life in residential homes for older people.

Following a severe and enduring episode of depression that lasted through 1997 to 2000, Tim Watkins began volunteering and later working for the charity Depression Alliance, running its Wales office, and steering it to becoming an independent charity in its own right in 2005. He continued to run the charity until 2010.

Between 2001 and 2010, the Welsh Government appointed him to sit on the *Health & Wellbeing Council for Wales* and the *Burrows-Greenwell Review of Mental Health in Wales*. He also played a key role in developing the *Healthy Minds at Work* project, during which he wrote *Taking Control*, an audio self-help book for people affected by depression, and oversaw the development of the award-winning *Depression Busting* self-management programme for people affected by depression.

In October 2010, along with Julia Kaye and Paul Clarke, Tim Watkins formed Life Surfing in order to address public wellbeing in people experiencing stress or whose life circumstances put them at risk of developing mental illness and people experiencing mild/moderate common mental illnesses such as anxiety and depression.

In addition to writing the growing range of Life Surfing publications, Tim Watkins, with Julia Kaye, has co-authored a range of training workshops:

- o *How to Help in a Crisis*: a one-day workshop for people who want to learn how to help and support people with mental health problems

- o *Distress to De-stress*: a 2 hour workshop for people who want to learn how to manage stress

- o *Getting to Sleep*: a 2 hour workshop for people experiencing stress-related sleep problems

- o *Banish your Blues*: a one-day workshop for people who want to learn how to self-manage depression

Tim Watkins provides one-to-one Wellbeing Coaching sessions to anyone that wants to improve their personal wellbeing either face-to-face at our consulting rooms in Cardiff or via Skype (please visit our website – www.life-surfing.com – for further information)

Foreword:

ABOUT SELF-HELP

Anyone who says that "self-help plays an important part in the treatment of depression" is 180 degrees wrong!

It is more correct to say that "treatment plays an important part in self-help for depression". This is because the overwhelming majority of people affected by depression recover using self-help alone. Most treatments are not "cures". They aim to give you the ability and motivation to engage in the self-help approaches that promote and sustain recovery.

For example, antidepressants bring about an improvement in mood and an increase in energy. This makes it easier to engage socially, be physically active, and to worry less. Similarly, talking therapies such as Counselling and Cognitive Behavioural Therapy encourage you to address your problems and engage in health-promoting behaviours such as socialising, physical activity and healthy eating.

So treatment fits within self-help. The relative importance of the two depends on the severity of your depression. Treatment may be unnecessary in mild depression, but will be essential in severe depression. But no matter how depressed you are, helping yourself is, in the end, the only road to sustained recovery.

So self-help is not an alternative to treatment. Rather, when it works for you, treatment can be an essential component without which, recovery may be delayed.

About depression

Depression is a common condition affecting around 23% of the population at some point in our lives.

Depression is diagnosed using a self-reporting questionnaire to determine how many of the symptoms of depression you are displaying, and how severe and enduring these symptoms are.

Almost all depression is reactive – it is a response to unpleasant life events that, for one reason or another, you are unable to deal with. The prognosis is excellent – 80% of people affected by depression recover without needing medical support. Of the remaining 20% who do need medical support (mostly counselling and antidepressants), almost all recover within six months.

Depression is a self-healing condition. That is, once you have come to terms with the unpleasant life events that triggered your depression, recovery is only a matter of time. How long recovery actually takes will depend on:

o   The extent to which you are doing things that get in the way of recovery (such as comfort eating or binge drinking)
o   Whether you are doing things that promote recovery (such as being socially and physically active, eating healthily, and regularly relaxing).

When thinking about depression, and when looking at any treatment, therapy or self-help practice, you should ask yourself:

o   Is this helping me to recover?

o   Does this make things worse?

This will vary from person to person. It will also help you to pick your way through the many debates and arguments that persist around depression. For example, there is a huge ongoing argument about whether antidepressants are a good or a bad thing. The truth is that while some people find them essential to recovery, others find them more unpleasant than depression itself. So the question is always, "how does this affect me personally?"

Tim Watkins

Symptoms and Warning Signs

Depression is not just feeling sad or unhappy. It is a potentially serious condition that has social, physical and psychological warning signs and symptoms.

Symptoms

The common symptoms of depression are:

o   Ongoing sadness and low mood
o   Feelings of helplessness and hopelessness
o   Tearfulness
o   Problems with sleep
o   Poor concentration and forgetfulness
o   Loss of enjoyment
o   Loss of sex drive
o   Changes in appetite and weight (usually loss of appetite and weight loss)
o   Feeling anxious or worried
o   Thoughts of self-harm or suicide.

Less common or less obvious symptoms include:
o   Physical aches and pains
o   Headaches
o   Digestive problems
o   Constipation
o   Changes to the menstrual cycle.

If you have several of these symptoms to the point that they are interfering with your daily life, for more than a fortnight, we recommend that you see your doctor. If you have thoughts of suicide or self-harm, we advise you to see your doctor. You might also want to talk confidentially to the Samaritans 08457 90 90 90.

Warning Signs

Although not strictly "symptoms" of depression, warning signs can be an early warning of the onset of depression. Knowing your warning signs is an essential part of self-help for depression. It can also help if you can share your warning signs with someone close to you (your partner, a friend, family member or work colleague) because sometimes other people are better placed to spot warning signs.

Warning signs vary from person to person, so it is important to think about any changes that happened as you became depressed. Warning signs can include any change in behaviour, but commonly include:

o   Using drugs like alcohol, caffeine and nicotine to dampen feelings of stress and anxiety
o   Comfort eating
o   Losing interest in our appearance (or becoming obsessively well turned out)
o   "Being busy" – using a lot of energy, but not actually getting things done
o   Withdrawing from social activities (making excuses to avoid people)
o   Developing a negative or pessimistic outlook on life
o   Struggling at work, school or college
o   Becoming forgetful.

Self-help approaches are much more effective when used during this "warning signs" stage or when depression is relatively mild. However, if depression becomes severe, some formal medical intervention will most probably be necessary to promote recovery.

Types of Depression

You may have heard that there are different types of depression, and may wonder about the difference between them. In fact, depression is a single condition. However, this is often obscured by medical jargon. There are also a few conditions that share some of the symptoms with depression.

Depression Jargon

Reactive Depression – Your depression developed as a reaction to a major life event such as a divorce or unemployment. Almost all episodes of depression are reactive.

Clinical Depression – This is not a statement of the severity or reality of your depression. All it means is that you have seen a doctor who has decided that your symptoms qualify for a diagnosis of depression.

Endogenous depression – This means "depression arising from within". This term has been used to describe depression where there is no obvious life event to explain it. However, in most cases, endogenous depression turns out to be the result either of a life event that has been overlooked or an underlying physical illness such as an under-active thyroid gland.

Mixed Anxiety and Depression – This diagnosis simply means that you have the symptoms of both depression and anxiety.

Treatment and self-help for depression is the same in each case, although to overcome anxiety some additional coping strategies may be needed.

Conditions with similar symptoms

Seasonal Affective Disorder (SAD) – About 1 person in 50 in the UK will have depression as a result of lack of sunlight in the winter months. A much larger group of people with depression also find that their symptoms worsen during the winter. Self-help solutions for SAD are very effective, and include the use of a light-box, changes to diet, and regular exercise.

Post Natal Depression – Lots of women experience "baby blues" – a brief period of low mood and tiredness. This usually goes away within a few weeks. A smaller number of women experience post natal depression, which is more profound and longer lasting.

Bipolar Affective Disorder (aka Bipolar Depression or Manic Depression) – This is a much rarer, and often more serious condition than (uni-polar) depression. Those affected can experience manic 'highs' as well as the symptoms of depression. It is important that this condition is not mistaken for depression, because the antidepressants often used to treat depression can trigger an episode of mania. Although self-management approaches are effective, more than 60% of people with this condition need to remain on mood stabilising medication.

Treating Depression

In recent years, doctors have also been encouraged to promote self-help approaches to depression. The treatment(s) you are offered will depend on the severity of your depression, your circumstances and access to support, and what treatments are available locally. The most common treatments are antidepressants and talking therapies (mainly Counselling or Cognitive Behavioural Therapy).

From a self-help perspective, you need to ask the same questions about formal treatments as you would of any approach. Remembering that depression is a self-healing condition:

"Is the treatment on offer going to speed up or stand in the way of my recovery?"

Most doctors will follow the treatment guidance set out by the National Institute for Health and Clinical Excellence (NICE), which recommends a "stepped care" approach that matches the intervention to the severity of your depression:

> Step 1: In all cases: carry out an assessment, provide information, encourage self-help, active monitoring with follow-up appointments, referral to other services where necessary.

> Step 2: Persistent symptoms that fall short of the threshold for depression together with mild to moderate depression: Counselling and other talking therapies, medication, active monitoring, referral to specialist services where necessary.

> Step 3: Persistent symptoms that fall short of the threshold for depression and mild to moderate depression where these fail to respond at step 2: Medication, high intensity

psychological therapies, combined treatments, referral to specialist services.

Step 4: Severe depression, risk of suicide or self-harm: Medication, high intensity psychological therapies, electroconvulsive therapy (ECT), crisis service, combined treatments, multi-professional and in-patient care.

Most people who seek treatment for depression are treated in primary care, usually using a combination of self-help approaches, counselling/talking therapies and medication (Steps 1 and 2). Very few are treated by specialist mental health teams or as in-patients in mental health units or hospitals (Steps 3 and 4).

Medication

Antidepressant medications are the most common and easily accessible treatment for depression.

Antidepressants have been found to be effective in 65-70% of people with depression. However, they are considerably less effective in people with mild depression than in those with the most severe depression.

There are currently around 30 different antidepressants available. These fall into 3 broad categories:

> *Tricyclic Antidepressants* (TCAs) have been around since the 1950s, but are still used today to treat moderate to severe depression. These drugs work by boosting the amounts of Serotonin and Noradrenaline in your nervous system. TCAs are as good as any other class of antidepressant, but can have unpleasant side effects and doses have to be precise to avoid overdose. As such, few GPs offer them as a first treatment for depression.

Selective Serotonin Reuptake Inhibitors (SSRIs) were first developed in the late 1970s, but became popular with the launch of Prozac in the mid-1980s. Fluoxetine (the generic name for Prozac) is still recommended by NICE as a first treatment for depression. SSRIs are no more effective than the older TCAs, but most users find them easier to tolerate. They are also safe even in relatively high overdose.

Monoamine Oxidase Inhibitors (MAOIs) are a less used class of antidepressant. Although they are at least as effective as other antidepressants, they can cause dangerous side effects. They can also be toxic when combined with the chemical tyramine, which is found in cured and fermented foods and drinks. Because of these complications, MAOIs are only used where other antidepressants have not been effective.

There are several other types of antidepressant that block the reuptake of Noradrenaline (NRI) or both Noradrenaline and Serotonin (SNRIs). There is also a new antidepressant, Agomelatin that blocks the reuptake of both Serotonin and the sleep hormone Melatonin. Because some newer antidepressants are significantly more expensive, they tend to be used only after a less costly SSRI has been tried.

When should you take an antidepressant?

There is not a hard and fast rule as to when you should take an antidepressant. However, if your depression has developed to the point that it interferes with your daily routine, you might want to consider taking an antidepressant – especially if you find that other approaches such as counselling and self-help have not helped.

Do antidepressants cure depression?

It is wrong to think of depression in the same way as we think of illnesses such as flu or measles. Similarly, it is wrong to expect antidepressants to work in the same way as antibiotics. A better comparison is with a plaster cast on a broken limb – giving support until you are ready to support yourself again.

Depression is the result of a complex interaction between an individual and his or her environment. There is no "cure" or "magic bullet". There are various treatments that either improve mood and energy levels or help you turn your life around. Most people find that a combination of treatments and self-help allow them to overcome depression.

Side Effects

Taking any medication carries a risk of side effects. It is important that you discuss these with your doctor or pharmacist: you need to read the patient information leaflet that comes with your antidepressant.

Be patient, the benefits of an antidepressant can take 3-4 weeks to kick in. Unfortunately, the side effects can start immediately (although they may wear off later). Only you can decide whether you can tolerate any side effects that you experience for long enough to see whether your depression improves.

Where the side effects outweigh the benefits, remember that there are many more antidepressants available. Don't be afraid to go back to your doctor to explain the side effects and ask for an alternative.

Withdrawal Symptoms

Around 60% of antidepressant users experience unpleasant side effects when they stop taking an antidepressant. This is especially true where antidepressants (such as Venlafaxine and Paroxetine) have a short "half-life" (the time taken for the dose of the drug in your system to halve). You can tell that these are withdrawal symptoms if they clear up when you take a dose of your antidepressant.

The antidepressants that your doctor is most likely to offer (Fluoxetine, Mirtazapine and Citalapram) are the ones with the longest half-life, and are thus the least likely to produce withdrawal symptoms.

Of those who do experience withdrawal, most have relatively mild symptoms that feel a bit like having a cold, and can simply stop taking their antidepressant. However, for a minority, withdrawal symptoms become so unpleasant that a process of "tapered withdrawal" is needed. Ordinarily, this will involve halving the dose every 3-7 days, and should take no more than 4 weeks. Only when withdrawal symptoms are severe should tapering last more than a month.

Are antidepressants addictive?

Although many people experience some degree of withdrawal symptoms, this does not mean that antidepressants are addictive.

Unlike users of addictive substances such as nicotine, people on antidepressants do not experience a craving for their antidepressant when they stop taking it. Nor do they need to constantly increase the dose of their antidepressant in order to get the desired improvement in their depression.

Talking Therapies

Depression is associated with distorted thinking and beliefs, and the unhelpful behaviours that follow. Talking therapies help promote recovery from depression by helping you understand and alter your thoughts, beliefs and behaviours.

There are three common types of talking therapies available through the NHS:

1. Counselling

2. Cognitive Behavioural Therapy (CBT)
3. Psychoanalytic and psychodynamic therapies.

Counselling helps you deal with immediate problems. You are encouraged to talk about what is happening to you and how you feel, and you are encouraged to find solutions. Counselling may be used both as a treatment for depression and as a means of staying mentally healthy. Counselling is usually time-limited (6 to 10 sessions).

Cognitive Behavioural Therapy (CBT) helps you unpick your thoughts, beliefs and behaviours, and to become more realistic/positive. CBT is the best researched talking therapy, but this does not mean that it is any more effective than any other therapy. CBT has been shown to be effective in the treatment of a range of mental health problems including depression, anxiety and obsessive compulsive disorder. CBT is usually time-limited (10 to 15 sessions).

Psychoanalytic and psychodynamic therapies involve a therapist listening to your experiences, exploring connections between present feelings and actions and past events. It aims to help you understand more about yourself and your relationships. Unlike Counselling and CBT, these therapies explore past events in detail in order to help you gain a deeper understanding of yourself.

Other, less common talking therapies that are available (in some areas) on the NHS include: cognitive analytic therapy, interpersonal psychotherapy and systemic therapy, humanistic and experiential psychotherapies, art therapy, music and drama therapy.

Safety Issues

Although talking therapies were promoted as a "safe" alternative to antidepressants, they are not risk-free. Focusing on your problems can make you feel worse. Therapy may adversely affect your relationships with loved ones, friends and work colleagues. You may become angry or feel vulnerable. You may feel worse before you feel better.

It is important that you discuss any side effects with the therapist.

Accessing Talking Therapies

Talking therapies are not immediately available. In most cases, you will need a referral from your GP. If you are assessed as needing therapy will you be put on the waiting list. This can mean a wait of several months between seeking help and receiving therapy.

In some areas you may be able to access CBT via the Improving Access to Psychological Therapies (IAPT) programme if you are out of work because of depression. However, waiting times will vary from area to area.

Some voluntary organisations (such as local Mind Associations) provide counselling services. The precise terms and conditions will vary – some offer a free service, some require a fee. Also, waiting times can vary.

The only way to guarantee immediate access to a talking therapy is to pay privately. The best starting point for finding a private therapist is to look at the British Association for Counselling and Psychological Therapies register.

Some health insurance policies cover psychological support, but many do not. You will need to check the small print. Also, the employee assistance programmes (EAPs) provided by larger companies may cover confidential psychological support – it is worth checking with your employer to see if they have an EAP in place.

Other Treatments

In recent years we have seen a range of new approaches to the treatment of depression. It is best to think of these in relation to the severity of depression they are intended to address.

Mild Depression

For mild depression, there have been several schemes that are not really "treatments", but formal attempts to promote healthier lifestyles. These include:

> *Bibliotherapy* or books on prescription schemes that allow doctors to "prescribe" from a range of approved self-help books, which can be picked up from the local library (even if you are not a member)

> *Exercise on prescription* schemes that allow doctors to refer you to a fitness coach at your local leisure centre. The coach will then work with you over 6-8 weeks to develop a fitness routine that you will then follow.

> *Ecotherapy* or working in green space schemes allow doctors to refer you to projects that involve work and/or recreation in open, green space.

Of course, you do not need to visit a doctor in order to read a self-help book, engage in physical activity or spend time in the open air. Indeed, many local charities and community groups offer such schemes to anyone who might benefit.

St. John's Wort has been shown to be more effective than antidepressants in the treatment of mild depression. It is not effective in more severe cases. Few UK doctors will prescribe St. John's Wort because the evidence for it is still inconclusive and because it can have side effects. Nevertheless, St John's Wort can be purchased as a traditional remedy for depression.

Moderate Depression

Most moderate depression is treated using a combination of medication and talking therapies. However, in some areas of the country you may be able to access less common treatments including:

Physiotherapy – can offer a 1-to-1 and more structured alternative to exercise on prescription.

Occupational Therapy – can offer 1-to-1 support with healthy and positive lifestyle changes

Art, Drama and Music Therapy – use art, drama and music to help you express how you feel, combined to talking therapies that allow you to overcome your depression.

Severe Depression

Where depression is particularly severe, and where a combination of antidepressants and psychological therapies has not helped, there are three relatively invasive approaches that can be offered:

Electroconvulsive Therapy (ECT) involves passing a small electric current through the brain. The procedure is carried out under general anaesthetic. The procedure is usually repeated twice a week for 3-6 weeks. ECT can be very effective in treating depression. However, because of its invasive nature and potential side effects, it is only used where conventional treatments have failed.

Transcranial Magnetic Stimulation (TMS) involves using a very powerful magnetic field to stimulate the brain. TMS has been shown to have some positive effect on severe depression, although it is not as effective as ECT. It has the advantage of being less invasive and has fewer side effects.

Vagus Nerve Stimulation (VNS) has been found to be effective in the treatment of severe depression, although there are concerns about its safety. VNS involves surgery to implant a device similar to a pacemaker into the left side of the chest, and to connect the electrodes to the left vagus nerve. Once in place, the device delivers an electric pulse that stimulates the nerve, and this, in turn helps reduce depression.

About self-help

Depression is a self-healing condition. Eighty percent of people affected by depression recover without need of medical support. Almost all of the remaining 20% recover within a year. This is because most of the stressful life events that trigger depression pass into history within a year. When you are worrying about the prospect of stressors like debt, divorce, redundancy, etc, it is easy to slip into the habits of depression:

o   Social withdrawal
o   Physical inactivity
o   Emotional numbness
o   Rumination
o   Negative thinking
o   Pessimism.

Often the imagined situation is worse than the reality. Also, once the situation has changed, it does not take long to adapt to the new circumstances. With time, the pain of loss and change disappears, and depression heals.

For most people, this happens by accident. But you can accelerate the process simply by learning which things promote self-healing and which things stand in its way. Unfortunately, this varies from person to person, so there are no shortcuts to learning what is going to work for you.

The key elements of self-help are:

o   Self-monitoring
o   Managing change/coping with loss
o   Avoiding quick-fixes
o   Making positive lifestyle choices.

Self-monitoring

A good starting point is to keep a self-monitoring diary in which you can track your mood and energy levels against a series of potentially helpful and unhelpful activities. That way you can see for yourself what works for you.

Managing change/coping with loss

Self-help includes addressing the stressful life events that trigger depression. Where possible, you should take action to come to terms with loss and change. This does not mean that you have to do it alone. A key self-help skill is to identify and engage with sources of help. For example, is you are having problems at work, you might want to talk to a trade union representative or an employment lawyer. Similarly, if you have experienced bereavement, you might want to contact Cruse Bereavement Care.

In some instances, you will be able to change the situation. In others, you will have to learn to adapt to the new situation.

Avoiding quick-fixes

As you become depressed, it is common to look for anything that will bring instant relief. Unfortunately, almost all the things that bring instant relief only do so in the short-term, and at the expense of further depression and worsening health in the long-term. For example, using alcohol can appear to have positive results such as:

o   You find socialising easier
o   You feel happier and less on edge
o   You find it easier to get to sleep.

But these are short-term results that you pay for in worsening depression and poorer general health.

Cutting down on quick-fixes and seeking lasting improvements for depression are the keys to self-help.

Making positive lifestyle choices

Simply avoiding quick-fixes is unlikely to work unless you are able to adopt healthy alternatives.

Unfortunately, many of the things that promote recovery from depression are "slow-fixes" because they do not appear to have much of an effect (or may even make you feel worse) in the short-term. But given time they will help you recover and avoid further episodes of depression. For example, research shows that physical activity is an effective "treatment" for depression. But if you haven't been active for some time, physical activity may leave you feeling exhausted, achy, breathless, etc. Indeed, overdo exercise at the beginning and you may find that your depression worsens for a few days. However, as your fitness levels improve, so your mood, energy levels and sleep patterns will improve too.

SELF-HELP TECHNIQUES 1:
SOCIAL ENGAGEMENT

Social withdrawal is one of the earliest and most common warning signs of depression.

Often you lose interest in things that you used to enjoy. Being with people is tiring and can leave you feeling down. It may seem easier to make an excuse than to force yourself to go out. The trouble is that once you've made an excuse, it is too easy to keep on making excuses. And the less you engage with people, the harder it becomes to re-engage.

Soon you are caught in another of depression's vicious circles, and need to find a way out.

Overcoming depression initially involves forcing yourself to re-engage with things that will eventually help you feel better, but doing so in ways that do not leave you tired and upset. Fortunately, there are things you can do for yourself:

1. **Spend time with people in short bursts**
2. **Be prepared to try new places/activities**
3. **Avoid using alcohol to make you feel sociable**
4. **Spend time with people who you know well enough to talk about how you feel**
5. **Be prepared to disengage when you get tired/down**
6. **Do not worry about being seen out if you are on sick leave**
7. **Do not feel under pressure to make conversation**
8. **Try to stay positive**
9. **Watch out for avoidance thoughts and behaviours.**
10. **Watch out for people/situations that leave you tired/negative**

1. Spend time with people in short bursts

Depression affects key social skills such as memory and concentration. This means that you have to spend more energy than normal just to follow a conversation – and it gets more difficult the more people are involved. So having a conversation with one person may be okay, but trying to converse with three or four people in a group may exhaust you. Unfortunately, if you become too tired, this will add to your depression later on.

It is helpful when you are recovering from depression to limit the time you spend with people to avoid over-tiring yourself. For example, having a coffee or a lunch hour with a friend may be okay, but spending the evening out with friends will be too much.

In time, so long as you avoid over-tiring yourself, you will find that you can build up the amount of time you can spend socialising.

2. Be prepared to try new places/activities

The tiredness and low mood that come with depression can make any activity seem to be a chore. It is all too easy to make excuses not to go out. But this means that you will be missing out on people, places and activities that would help your recovery.

Being open to new activities and new places will help you discover things that promote recovery – use the monitoring form (see above) to keep track of things that help and things that hinder recovery.

3. Avoid using alcohol to make you feel sociable

You might be tempted to use alcohol to aid social engagement. Alcohol is readily available, and many social venues and events involve drinking. This may leave you feeling pressured to drink more than you would want.

In small quantities, alcohol can:

o   Help overcome shyness and anxiety
o   Make you feel more sociable

o Increase your confidence
o Make you more relaxed.

Unfortunately, these "benefits" only come with very small quantities of alcohol. Also, alcohol is a depressant drug that will make your depression worse. It will also impact on your physical health, adding to your feelings of tiredness.

While you are recovering from depression, it is important that you drink as little alcohol as possible.

4. Spend time with people who you know well enough to talk about how you feel

Being able to talk about your feelings can be a big help when you are recovering from depression. Sadly, this is not always easy. Your relatives and friends may want to help, but may not know what to do. Many people are so afraid of doing the wrong thing that they end up doing nothing at all.

This said, you may be pleasantly surprised if you do decide to tell someone that you have depression. More than 20% of the population have experienced depression, so many of us have either had the condition ourselves or have a friend or family member who has been through it.

You may well have friends or family members who will want to help you recover from depression. If you can give them information about self-help, they can become a valuable resource to help you overcome your depression.

5. Be prepared to disengage when you get tired/down

Tiredness is one of the biggest barriers to recovery from depression. Recovery means working at your own pace through a gradual process back to wellbeing. Doing too much today will leave you feeling more depressed tomorrow.

Letting people know that you may get tired will give you a degree of control over your situation. For example, if you are going out with friends, you might start by telling them that you don't want to stay out late. This will allow you to leave early if you feel yourself getting tired. Similarly, if you invite people to your home, you could set a time limit on it – eg, inviting them around for an hour.

Like any other activity, when you are recovering from depression you need to build yourself up gradually. By respecting yourself when you feel tired at the beginning of your recovery, you will gradually be able to do more and more.

6. Don't worry about being seen out if you are on sick leave

If you are on sick leave or claiming sickness benefits, you may be worried about being seen out and about. You may worry that your employer or the DWP will not believe that you are ill and that some sanction will be taken against you. You have rights in employment and (if your depression is long-term) disability law that you can use to prevent either acting against you.

Getting plenty of daylight and fresh air, and being socially and physically active are known to promote recovery. Indeed, your doctor will encourage you to do these things. Your employer will also want you to engage in these activities if they will help you return to work.

If need be, ask your doctor to add these activities to your medical record as part of what you need to do to treat your depression.

7. Don't feel under pressure to make conversation

While you are depressed, you will be less able to do things that you would ordinarily take for granted. Because of the way depression affects your memory and concentration, you may find engaging in conversation difficult and tiring – particularly if you are trying to follow a group conversation.

You may feel that you have to participate. However, you should try to respect yourself when you feel tired. Rather than forcing yourself to speak, it is okay just to listen and let others do the talking.

8. Try to stay positive

In the early stages of recovery, and particularly if your depression is severe, you may feel that no amount of social engagement is working for you. It is important to stay positive rather than withdraw still further.

Often, the feeling that you are not getting anywhere will be because:

o   You are overdoing things and ending up exhausted
o   You are getting some small benefits but these are not yet noticeable.

You could try using a monitoring form (see above) to work out which people/places/activities are best for your recovery. You could also try to limit the time you spend on social activity then gradually build this up.

9. Watch out for avoidance thoughts and behaviours

Depression changes the way you think and the things you believe. In general, depression will make you pessimistic and cause you to believe that you will never recover. You will find similar types of thoughts and beliefs arise in relation to the various things you are doing to try to recover.

For example, you might go out with friends, but end up overdoing it, and feeling tired and low the following day. You might then find yourself thinking that "trying to engage socially makes no difference". You might believe that you are better off staying at home in order to overcome tiredness and low mood.

It is important to understand that this is not "the truth", but is impaired thinking caused by your depression.

Rather than give in to thoughts and beliefs that would cause you to withdraw still further (thus making your depression even worse) try being a bit more systematic about re-engaging. Observe what it is you do so that you avoid things that tire you, and start off slowly (for example, meet someone for an hour rather than a night out) and build up gradually at your own pace.

10. Watch out for people / situations that leave you tired / negative

There are some people and some situations that leave you feeling positive and energised. Others leave you feeling tired and negative. When you are recovering from depression, you should try to spend time with people or in situations that leave you feeling positive and energised.

By monitoring how you feel following social engagement, you can identify those people and situations that leave you positive and energised and those that leave you tired and negative. This will help you decide when you should engage socially.

Self-Help Techniques 2:
PHYSICAL ACTIVITY

The physical side of depression has often been overlooked because of the current fashion to focus on treating thoughts and beliefs. However, if you have depression you are probably as concerned about not sleeping and feeling exhausted during the day as you are about feeling sad. Having depression often results in deteriorating physical health because:

o   Social withdrawal leads to a sedentary lifestyle
o   Tiredness makes you inactive
o   Comfort eating leads to weight gain
o   Stress results in aches, pains, headaches and digestive problems.

Regular physical activity can overcome the symptoms of depression. Indeed, exercise is a "wonder drug" for many conditions including depression. Below are 10 things you can do to get physically active:

11. **Get a daily dose of daylight and fresh air**
12. **Being active doesn't have to be expensive**
13. **Any activity will do!**
14. **Stop when you feel tired**
15. **Take physical activity in small steps – build up to 30 minutes a day**
16. **Re-engage with activities you used to enjoy, and be open to new things**
17. **Get into a routine**
18. **Team up with an exercise buddy (or get a dog!)**
19. **Join a club or exercise class**
20. **Get a health check if you have been inactive for some time.**

11. Get a daily dose of daylight and fresh air

It is all too easy to hide yourself away indoors when you are depressed. So just getting out of the house can be a first step on the road to recovery from depression.

Getting out does not mean jumping straight into vigorous exercise. If you have been inactive for some time, just spending time in the garden, visiting a local park, walking to the nearest shop or walking around the block is enough.

The important thing is that you make time every day to get some daylight and fresh air.

12. Being active doesn't have to be expensive

Many people say they cannot afford to be physically active. This is because we have been conditioned to think that you have to join a gym, health centre or sports club. In fact, being physically active can be as cheap or expensive as you decide.

If you do not have the money, you could take up walking or jogging. Walking and jogging are free, underestimated and not what we are used to doing.

In some areas, there are also charities that recycle bicycles, so taking up cycling can be done on a budget. If you do want to try gym-based activities, find out if your local authority provides free or discounted access to leisure centres for people on low incomes. Alternatively, in some areas the NHS operates "exercise on prescription" schemes that you may be able to do for free.

13. Any activity will do !

There are broadly two types of physical – aerobic exercise (e.g., running) and stretching exercise (e.g., Pilates). Ideally, you should try to engage in both. However, it is particularly important to engage in an aerobic exercise (that leaves you out of breath) for 20-30 minutes at least 3 days per week – although you may have to build up to this.

What makes you breathless will depend on how fit you are. If you have not been active for some time, just walking up and down stairs a few times may be sufficient to raise your heart and breathing rate. If you are more active, you may need a brisk walk, jog or cycle ride.

So, find something – anything – that you enjoy (or used to enjoy) that raises your heart and breathing rate, and build it into your weekly activity.

14. Stop when you feel tired

When you are recovering from depression, it is important to respect your body. A big barrier to recovery is overdoing things at the beginning. If your system is overworked, this can leave you feeling depressed for the next few days, and will negate the benefits of being active.

The ideal is to engage in 30 minutes of aerobic exercise, but you may find that you can only do 5 or 10. If this is the case, stop and rest.

15. Take physical activity in small steps – build up to 30 minutes a day

Engaging in physical activity as you recover from depression is like training for a marathon. Rather than try (and fail) to do 26 miles, you start by doing a few hundred metres and then build up gradually.

So, start with what you can do, and build up week by week. In part, this can be by adding to what you are already doing. For example, if you began by walking for a mile, you might try 2 miles next week. In part, it can be adding different activities. For example, if you started walking on Mondays, you could try cycling or swimming on Wednesdays.

16. Re-engage with activities you used to enjoy, and be open to new things

Because depression causes you to lose interest in things that you used to enjoy, it is easy to believe that you will not enjoy them in future. But re-engaging with them is a useful step on the road to recovery because as your depression lifts, so your sense of enjoyment will return.

It can also help to try out new things rather than dismiss them because your depression has caused you to believe that you will not enjoy them. This can be particularly true where there is a social element to the activity, such as a team sport.

17. Get into a routine

It is important to get into a habit of being physically active, so that it becomes just something you do, not something that you need to go out of your way to do.

If you are in work, this might appear daunting as you might think that there are not enough hours in the day to do exercise. Also, the last thing you feel like doing after a hard day is to go out again to do exercise. But it can be quite easy to build exercise into your daily routine:

- o If you use public transport, you could get off at the stop before work (or home) and walk for the remainder of your journey.
- o If you live quite close to your work, you could swap your car for a bicycle – in congested cities this may not be much slower (and is cheaper) than the car.
- o If you drive, try stopping off at a gym or swimming pool as part of your commute.
- o If you can develop an exercise routine, you will eventually find yourself just doing it without thinking and without having to motivate yourself – even on those days when you do not feel up to it.

18. Team up with an exercise buddy (or get a dog !)

Motivating yourself to be active can be difficult, particularly when you are starting out. Also, your depression can cause you to avoid doing things even when you know they are good for you.

If you find that you need a little extra motivation to get physically active, a very effective method is to team up with someone. You are less likely to withdraw if you have arranged to meet your exercise buddy – or if you are sharing a lift. And you will probably be helping them on the days when they don't feel like exercising.

If you are an animal person, getting a dog will also force you to go out for a walk, whatever the weather and no matter how you feel. Your dog will simply follow you, lead in mouth, pestering you until you take him out for his walk. Owning a dog can also be a spur to social engagement, as other dog owners are more likely to engage in conversation.

19. Join a club or exercise class

Joining a club or exercise class can also provide additional motivation to exercise, and can become a social activity too. However, you should only consider this option if you are sure you are going to attend, and if you are sure you can afford the entry fees.

If you are just starting your recovery, joining a club might seem like the right thing to do. But you may be biting off more than you can chew if it means that you overdo things and then become too tired to engage again. Also, many clubs charge a high joining fee and insist on your taking out a long membership contract. This can be a lot of money if you end up not using the club regularly. As such, you should think about trying cheaper alternatives such as walking, running, cycling and swimming before paying to join a club.

Exercise classes are less expensive. Some even operate on a drop-in basis, so you only pay for the classes you attend. However, if they prove too much and you end up dropping out, this may lower your mood and make you less likely to stick with physical activity. Again, you should think about whether you are really ready to do a class before signing up.

20. Get a health check if you have been inactive for some time

If you have not been active for some time, particularly if you are over 40 or if you have other illnesses or disability as well as depression, you should get a health check done before engaging in exercise. You can get a "Health MOT" type check through your GP. There are also several pharmacies that offer health checks that will include:

o   Blood pressure
o   Cholesterol
o   Diabetes
o   Lung efficiency
o   Weight check.

If you do have any problems, your doctor will be able to advise you on the type and degree of activity you should engage in. Your doctor may also be able to refer you to a physiotherapist or an exercise on prescription scheme to help you develop a personalised exercise programme.

Self-Help Techniques 3:
SLEEP

Depression and disrupted sleep are bound up together. Disrupted sleep is both a cause and a symptom of depression. As a result, you can easily get into a downward spiral of sleeplessness which makes your depression worse.

You may well experience disrupted sleep in four ways:

o   Being unable to get to sleep – often lying awake "ruminating" (worrying over and over) and being unable to switch your mind off

o   Vivid dreaming when you eventually get to sleep

o   Waking in the early hours – your mind is wide awake but your body feels drained

o   Daytime tiredness – you may feel exhausted and your mind is slow.

It is important to understand that this is part of a depression-sleep spiral that can cause you to become seriously depressed unless you take active steps to break the habitual pattern.

Fortunately, there is a long list of things that you can do to break out of your disrupted sleep pattern:

21. **Avoid caffeine after 6.00pm**
22. **Avoid stimulating activities before bed**
23. **Avoid using alcohol or sleeping pills to get to sleep**
24. **Get into a bedtime routine**
25. **Keep the bedroom clean, quiet and comfortable**
26. **Don't sleep during the day**
27. **Don't take work to bed**
28. **Don't worry if you cannot sleep**
29. **Keep a notepad by the bed**
30. **Don't have clocks in the bedroom.**

21. Avoid caffeine after 6.00pm

Caffeine is the active drug within an array of common drinks (coffee, tea, cola, iron bru), energy drinks, chocolate and some medicines (particularly cold and flu remedies). Caffeine helps you stay awake and alert for several hours after it is consumed.

If you are struggling to get to sleep at night, it is a good idea to avoid caffeine (and other stimulants) altogether. However, if you do have to have caffeine, try to restrict it to mornings. At the very least, do not have caffeine after 6.00pm unless you do not intend to go to bed until midnight!

You might want to avoid consuming sugar during the evening as this can give you a burst of energy just at the time when you want to be unwinding.

22. Avoid stimulating activities before bed

Ideally, the hour or so before bed time should be a period of relaxation. But in our busy, 24 hour society, it is easy to try to cram in as many activities as we can.

If you are not sleeping, it is important to look at the things you do before bed time. Are you relaxing and unwinding? Or are you up until late watching TV, playing computer games or doing work around the house?

23. Avoid using alcohol or sleeping pills to get to sleep

Drugs provide a common quick-fix for poor sleep. Visit your doctor and you may well be offered:

o   A hypnotic sleeping drug
o   A tranquiliser
o   A sleep-promoting antidepressant.

A glass of whisky or brandy before bed is a more traditional remedy for poor sleep.

Unfortunately, while these approaches help you get to sleep, they provide poor quality sleep. Often they result in your remaining in the shallow sleep that most people experience in the early stages of sleep. They provide less of the REM Sleep and Deep Sleep that is needed to refresh mind and body.

You will build up a tolerance to all of these substances so that in time you will need more in order to get to sleep. You will also find it difficult to sleep without the substance. Tranquilisers are particularly dangerous in this respect, as they are highly addictive. Alcohol is also addictive, and can seriously damage your health in the long term.

24. Get into a bedtime routine

If you've ever tried to get to sleep early because you need to be up for something the following day, you will know that getting to sleep is more than an act of will. Most times when you go to bed early, you have a frustrating time not being able to get off to sleep. Indeed, you may even end up getting to sleep later than if you had stuck to your normal bedtime.

This inability to sleep can be partly explained by worry about whatever you have to be up early for. But another important reason is that we wake and sleep according to circadian rhythms and our internal biological clock. These, in turn, are influenced partly by habit and partly by external cues such as light, temperature and noise.

Your body clock can be reset – someone who experiences jet lag when they travel to a different time zone will eventually adjust to the new time. But resetting your body clock takes time and practice.

Developing and sticking to a new bedtime routine will help you reset your body clock, making it easier to get to sleep.

Your routine should involve relaxing and unwinding activities in the run up to bed time. You should also try to address some of the cues that affect your body clock such as:

Light – if you live in a city, you may need dark curtains to fully darken your bedroom. You might also find that dimming the lights before bedtime will help you relax.

Temperature – if your bedroom is too hot, this will interfere with your ability to sleep.

Noise – if you cannot escape noise altogether, you might want to think about getting some earplugs.

Eating an hour earlier can also help change the body clock. This will be particularly helpful if you have got into a habit of eating quite late in the evening.

Once you have developed your routine, stick with it. It will take time, but doing the same things night after night will help you get back into the habit of sleeping.

25. Keep the bedroom clean, quiet and comfortable

Your bedroom should be somewhere that you want to go to at the end of a stressful day – not somewhere that gives you a feeling of guilt because you haven't tidied up for some time.

A cluttered room will be uncomfortable, and will prevent you sleeping. So making sure you only have essential things in the bedroom, and that you tidy regularly is important.

Ideally, you should not have distractions like computers, TVs, clocks or phones in the bedroom, as psychologically, these condition you to think of the bedroom as an ordinary living area rather than the private space where you go to sleep.

It is important that the bedroom is ventilated (much better than smelling of stale sheets!), warm but not too hot, quiet and dark.

26. Don't sleep during the day

If you are experiencing disrupted sleep, then you are bound to feel exhausted during the day. You will face a huge temptation to try to "catch up on sleep" during the day, especially if you are on sick leave or out of work.

Unfortunately, sleeping during the day does little to overcome your feeling of tiredness, and makes it much harder to sleep at night.

Even if you haven't slept during the night, it is important to get up, shower and have breakfast – this is part of the routine that will reset your body clock so that you can get to sleep later on.

Getting daylight and fresh air, and moving your body will help relieve some of your feeling of tiredness, so find something you can do that involves leaving the house. You might:

o   Go for a walk in a local park
o   Walk to the shops
o   Do some work in the garden
o   Wash the car.

Being physically active will ward off the feeling of tiredness and will help you sleep at night. You might want to think about joining a gym or a fitness class – if you are out of work, you may be entitled to free or discounted access to a local leisure centre. If you are being treated for depression, you might be eligible for an "exercise on prescription" programme.

If you do have to sleep in the day, try "power napping" (taking about 20 minutes of sleep) rather than allowing yourself to sleep indefinitely – use an alarm clock to make sure you wake up after 20 minutes.

27. Don't take work to bed

Taking work to bed can mean both actually working while in bed (perhaps reading papers and reports) or psychologically working (perhaps thinking about workplace problems). Both of these practices will prevent you from sleeping.

If your work is so pressured that you are actually working late into the evening, or even taking work to bed, you will have to think about how you are going to address this problem. If you are able to, you should raise your concerns with your employer – your employer has a duty of care not to endanger your health, so it is important that you put on record that you are under pressure to work at home. If you are in a trade union or if there is a recognised trade union in your workplace, they may be able to negotiate a reduction in your workload.

If you are unable to get your employer to reduce your workload, you need to consider whether you are in the right occupation – although unemployment is currently high, there are jobs around, and most employers prefer to take on someone who is already in work than someone who is on benefits. It might be that a change of job, with less pressure would be better for your health.

If you are psychologically working you need to look at how effective this is. Most of us forget the things we think about before we go to sleep. Also, the ideas that we have when we are tired tend not to be particularly good ones. Rather than simply allowing yourself to worry, add thinking about your work to your evening routine – take time out to write down the things that are worrying you together with any solutions you might have. Then leave them for the following day!

28. Don't worry if you cannot sleep

Not sleeping can become yet another thing to worry about as you lie in bed trying to get to sleep. The longer it takes to get off to sleep, the more you worry about not getting enough sleep.

Actually, we all under-estimate the amount of sleep we get because when we are asleep (even during light sleep) we are not aware of the passage of time. During the time that you think you are lying awake, you are probably falling in and out of sleep.

If you cannot get off to sleep, try to look at why this is. Are you physically uncomfortable? Or are you ruminating? Most physical discomfort can be dealt with – for example, if you are too hot, turn the heating down, use less bedding or open a window.

If you are ruminating, you need to slow your mind down. You can do this by practising relaxation techniques that help you to focus on your body or your breathing.

If things are particularly bad and even relaxation techniques don't help, get up and do something! If you are going to be awake anyway, do something productive around the house until you begin to feel tired again. Once you feel tired, go back to bed and try to sleep again.

29. Keep a notepad by the bed

Trying to remember things that you are worried about becomes yet another worry that stands in the way of sleep. Keeping a notepad and pen next to the bed is an effective way of minimising this.

When something is worrying you, write it down and come back to it in the morning. The odds are that when you come back to the things you have written, they will not seem as troubling as they did when you were lying awake during the night. Also, any decisions that you need to make in response to your worries will be much better after you have slept than when you are lying awake tired.

It is psychologically important that you do go back to the things you write during the night. Over time your mind will learn that it is okay not to worry about something once it has been written down, as you will revisit it later.

30. Don't have clocks in the bedroom

You probably need an alarm clock to help you get up in time for work in the morning. If you are not sleeping, the need for an alarm clock is even greater – it is all too easy to roll over for an extra five minutes sleep, only to find that you sleep for an hour or more.

Unfortunately, having a clock in the bedroom makes you aware of the passage of time, and gives you something else to worry about. If you wake in the early hours, and turn to look at the clock, this will remind you of how few hours sleep you have had, and how few hours remain before you have to get up again.

If you cannot easily see a clock, you are more likely to roll over and go back to sleep.

If possible, don't have a clock in the bedroom at all. If you need an alarm, try putting the clock immediately outside the bedroom door (where you can hear it but not see it). If you must have the clock in your bedroom, put it somewhere out of reach and facing away from you.

If your clock is out of reach, this has the added advantage that you are forced to get out of bed to turn the alarm off in the morning. Once up, it is easier to shower, dress and get breakfast rather than go back to a warm bed.

Self-Help Techniques 4:
STRESS AND RELAXATION

All of us experience stress to some extent. In an emergency, stress can be a life saver. In less dramatic situations, stress can help improve your performance. But too much stress over too long a period of time is dangerous.

Most depression is triggered by too much stress over too long a period of time. Once triggered, depression lowers your ability to cope with stress. This results in a vicious circle in which each new stressor makes you more depressed, making you even less able to cope. In the end, you may find yourself giving up on life – no longer going out, avoiding people, not answering phone calls or opening letters.

There are three key ways in which you can manage stress, and increase your resilience to stress:

o Talking (social engagement)
o Physical activity
o Relaxation.

There are separate chapters (above) for the first two of these. This chapter will help you learn to relax:

31. Learn to take action and minimise rumination
32. Be aware of your body
33. Be aware of your breathing
34. Avoid over-use of stimulants
35. Make time and space for relaxation
36. Try complementary therapies
37. Engage in activities that help you de-stress
38. Use a relaxation CD or mp3
39. Join a relaxation class
40. Keep a sense of proportion.

31. Learn to take action and minimise rumination

You may well find that you spend a lot of time "ruminating" (worrying over and over about things you can do nothing about). The only result of this is to make you even more depressed – it is the mental equivalent of poking an aching tooth with your tongue!

It can help to challenge your worries. This will help you put them into perspective and separate those that require action from those you can do nothing about.

32. Be aware of your body

If you are depressed, you will find that most of your conscious attention is focused on your thoughts and feelings. You are much less likely to be conscious of what is happening to your body. This means that you are not picking up important warning signs of stress. It also prevents you from taking early action to avoid health problems.

By taking time to focus on how your body is, you will notice:

o   *Your posture* – this will be crouched (think of a boxer's stance) if you are stressed
o   *Your breathing* – this will be fast, shallow, and based at the top of the chest if you are stressed
o   *Areas of tension* – you are likely to have headaches, stomach aches and muscle aches and pains when you are stressed.

Once you are aware of what is happening to your body, you can take steps to improve things:

o   straightening your posture by stretching upward
o   bringing your breath down to your belly and breathing deeper and slower
o   relaxing the muscles associated with any aches and pains.

You may find the exercises used in Tai Chi and Yoga helpful in de-stressing your body.

33. Be aware of your breathing

Ideally, your breathing should be slow and deep, with the breath focused on your belly so that you are using the whole of your lungs. Anxiety, depression and stress tend to cause the breath to be fast and shallow and focused on the upper chest – the opposite of healthy breathing, and ultimately a contributory factor in illness and disease.

Aerobic exercise is useful in correcting your breathing, as the exertion involved will force your body to use the whole of the lung to take in sufficient oxygen to keep going. However, aerobic exercise is not a guarantee of relaxation.

The breathing techniques used in Yoga aid relaxation by encouraging the body to use the whole lung to breathe deeply and slowly. A simple example of this type of exercise is:

o   Sit comfortably somewhere quiet where you will not be disturbed
o   Place one hand on your belly, just below the navel
o   Place the other hand on the breast bone at the centre of your chest
o   Now close your eyes and focus your attention on your hands
o   Imagine that as you breathe in, the hand on your belly is pushed outward, and the hand on your chest is pushed upward and outward.

This exercise will help you pull your breath down into the lower part of your lungs.

34. Avoid over-use of stimulants

People who are stressed will use stimulants such as caffeine and nicotine to help alleviate the effects of stress. Unfortunately, substance use of this kind is a classic "quick-fix" – it gives short-term relief at the cost of long-term health problems.

Stimulants make it harder for you to relax and unwind. They are also a cause of anxiety, and may trigger panic attacks – particularly if you are using them regularly.

35. Make time and space for relaxation

You may well object that you haven't got time to relax. However, few of us are able to relax for more than a few minutes at a time. It is difficult to argue that you don't have 5 minutes in the course of a day!

Ideally, you should set aside the same time every day for relaxation – and let people around you know that this is "me time".

Ideally, you should use or create a quiet space for relaxation. This could be a spare room or, in summer, the garden or a seat in a local park.

36. Try complementary therapies

If you struggle to relax, and find that simple self-help techniques are not enough, you could consider complementary therapies such as: aromatherapy, massage, reflexology, shiatsu, etc. You might need to try different therapies and therapists to find something that suits you.

Although there is little evidence in favour of these therapies as a treatment for illness, they are very useful in managing stress and promoting relaxation. This, in turn, can be an important component of recovery from depression.

37. Engage in activities that help you de-stress

All of us have activities that help us unwind. Unfortunately, when you are depressed, you can lose interest. You may also find that you seem to derive less benefit from them. However, if you can continue to engage, you will find that they gradually help lift your depression.

De-stress activities vary from person to person, and are not just physical activities. Arts and crafts can help. So too can gardening, walking, reading, etc. It is a matter of trying things out to see what you enjoy most.

38. Use a relaxation CD or mp3

You might find that a relaxation CD or mp3 will help you relax. These aids to relaxation come in two forms:

o   Relaxing music or sounds
o   Someone talking you into a relaxation.

You will need to experiment to find which approach works best for you.

39. Join a relaxation class

You may be able to find a relaxation class in your area. These classes will explore a range of relaxation and de-stress approaches.

Alternatively, you might want to try classes in:

o   Meditation
o   Mindfulness
o   Tai Chi
o   Yoga.

Each of these also involves a relaxation component as well as helping you de-stress.

40. Keep a sense of proportion

Don't let your worries make you so stressed that they take over your life. Your depression will make you believe that the smallest of concerns is a really big deal. Indeed, if you are depressed your system will often experience a feeling of anxiety, and then look for something to worry about.

Often your worries will be unfounded. Be aware of whether your thinking is distorted. Are you crystal ball gazing – making predictions about how bad the future will be, even though nobody can know the future?

Is there plausible evidence to back up your worries, or are you "catastrophising"? As the ancient Chinese proverb says:

" *The road ahead is smooth. Why are you throwing rocks on it?*"

Self-Help Techniques 5:
DIET AND DEPRESSION

Poor diet is both a cause and a consequence of depression. Poor diet can cause or worsen depression by making you feel generally less healthy, less energised and more lethargic. Poor diet can also be a consequence of depression because:

o   You comfort eat with sugary foods and chocolate
o   Antidepressants produce cravings for starchy food
o   Social withdrawal and anxiety prevent you from visiting supermarkets and markets
o   You lack the energy and motivation to prepare and cook fresh foods.

Reversing this process and adopting a healthy diet can have a big impact on your mood. Taking some simple steps can help:

41. **Avoid comfort eating**
42. **Try to eat 5 a day**
43. **Keep your diet balanced and varied**
44. **Try to avoid processed foods**
45. **Drink 6 glasses of fluid a day**
46. **Healthy eating isn't expensive**
47. **Healthy eating doesn't take time**
48. **Learn to cook!**
49. **Experiment with good mood foods**
50. **Watch out for salt and sugar.**

41. Avoid comfort eating

The stress that accompanies depression can lead to cravings for chocolate and sugary foods like cake and sweets. Also, some antidepressants can cause cravings for sweet and starchy food. This can give you the feeling that you are hungry when you are not.

If you have strong willpower, you may be able simply to resist the temptation to eat. Most of us can't. Instead, you could try:

o   Drinking when you feel hungry – we sometimes mistake thirst for hunger, so you may actually need water. Even if you don't, drinking a glass of water will help fill your stomach and ease any feeling of hunger

o   Substitute healthier foods – try eating fruit or raw vegetables instead of chocolate and cake.

o   Try smaller portions – on those occasions when you do have chocolate or cake, try to cut down on the amount you eat.

o   Spend time outdoors – when you are out, you will be less tempted to eat, and you will have less access to food

o   Don't keep comfort food in the house – if you don't buy chocolate, biscuits, cake or sweets, then comfort eating will involve having to go to the shops. This gives you a chance to overcome any passing craving.

42. Eat 5 a day

Eating 5 portions of fruit and vegetables every day is a measure of a healthy diet. A portion is roughly the size of an average clenched fist, or the size of a medium apple.

Eating 5 portions a day can be quite difficult – particularly as potatoes don't count! But there are some surprising foods that do count. There are three portions of vegetables in a full English breakfast – baked beans, mushrooms and tomatoes. This goes up to four if you also have a glass of fruit juice.

Remember that eating 5 a day is a target to aim for, not a necessity – don't beat yourself up if you only manage 3 or 4.

43. Keep your diet balanced and varied

Varying your diet means trying to introduce new foods into your meals every day so that you increase the chances of getting all of the nutrients, vitamins and minerals that your body needs. Balancing your diet means getting the right proportion of fruit and vegetables, carbohydrates, proteins and fats so that you are not eating too many harmful substances and not causing your body to put on extra weight.

Ideally, vegetables and fruit should make up a third of your diet. A further third should be bread, cereals and other complex carbohydrates like potatoes, rice and pasta. The remainder of your diet should be almost a sixth for milk and dairy products, and almost a sixth for meat, fish and other proteins. The remaining sliver is for fatty comfort foods like chocolate, ice cream and cake.

44. Try to avoid processed foods

If you are depressed, it can be very tempting to buy foods that are nearly ready to eat, such as instant noodles or rice, or microwave pies or ready meals. While these are easy to prepare, they often contain large quantities of unhealthy fats, sugar and salt, and only small amounts of healthy fats, complex carbohydrates, proteins and vegetables.

It is much better to prepare food from fresh ingredients. This does not have to be expensive or time consuming if you learn to prepare fast healthy meals such as salads, stir fries, pasta dishes and rice dishes. Indeed, even meat, potatoes and mixed vegetables can be ready within 15 minutes!

If you do buy ready meals, a good rule is that if you can tell what the ingredients are by looking, then the meal is relatively healthy (although you still need to look out for high levels of salt and fat). So, if you can see pieces of meat or vegetables it is significantly better than a puree or a pie.

45. Drink 6 glasses of fluid a day

Getting dehydrated can cause your depression to worsen.

It is important to get enough fluid every day to improve your mood, energy levels and general sense of wellbeing. For the average person, this means drinking about 6 glasses of fluid (about 3 pints) every day.

Other than alcoholic drinks, anything you drink counts toward your 6 a day. Alcohol doesn't because it is a diuretic. So, tea, coffee, fruit juice and squash also count.

46. Healthy eating isn't expensive

One of the main objections people with depression make is that healthy eating is expensive. This is a particular issue if you are on sick leave or on benefits.

In practice, the packaging and preparation involved in unhealthy foods often makes them more expensive than raw ingredients. The trick is to know where and when to shop for healthy raw ingredients.

If you use a supermarket, find out if there are particular days and times when they reduce the price of perishable foods – you may be able to buy meat, vegetables and fruit for half the price if you do this. Alternatively, you may find that markets, barrows, butchers, fishmongers and greengrocers can offer cheaper raw ingredients – it is largely about being prepared to take what is on offer on the day.

Basing meals around rice, pasta or boiled/baked potatoes is a good way of getting a cheap, healthy and filling meal.

47. Healthy eating doesn't take time

Another objection when you are depressed is that preparing healthy food takes too long – when you are depressed, you just can't be bothered!

Actually, within 15 minutes you can easily prepare:

o   A salad
o   A stir fry
o   A pasta meal

o   A rice dish
o   Fried or grilled meat, potatoes and mixed vegetables.

You could also try preparing and freezing soup, chilli, curry, Bolognese, etc so that they can be heated in a microwave and be ready to eat with rice or pasta within 15 minutes.

48. Learn to cook !

Of course, you might not be able to cook (or at least, you may not think you can). In fact, it is really easy to chop and boil some vegetables, grill some meat and boil up some potatoes. And it takes no time at all to flavour these with a pour-over sauce or gravy.

The first step is to find a cookery class in the area where you live. Try searching Google for "cookery classes" or contact your local council.

49. Experiment with good mood foods

In recent years there has been growing interest in foods containing substances that have antidepressant properties, such as Omega 3 oils and tryptophan. While not getting enough of these substances has been shown to make your depression worse, the jury is out on whether eating these foods can treat depression.

On the bright side, though, many of the good mood foods containing these ingredients are healthy in their own right. So eating them as part of a balanced and varied diet is certainly not going to harm you. You may well find that they help to lift your mood and energy levels.

50. Watch out for salt, sugar and sweeteners

One of the symptoms of depression is losing your senses of smell and taste. Food that you used to enjoy may taste bland, and this can remove the enjoyment of eating. Because of this, it is tempting to opt for strong flavoured foods. And while this isn't necessarily unhealthy, you need to beware of food that contains too much salt, sugar or artificial sweeteners.

Salt is bad for your general health, and is a major cause of high blood pressure and heart disease. Too much can affect your general health too. Sugar can give you an instant energy "hit", but only at the cost of lower mood and tiredness for the rest of the day. Too much can cause you to put on weight, adding to your tiredness and depression.

Some research suggests that the chemicals used in artificial sweeteners may cause or worsen depression. It is a good idea to avoid too many artificial sweeteners (although these days the food industry uses these instead of sugar because they are cheaper).

If you need to find foods with strong flavours, experiment with pepper and spices instead of sugar and salt.

Self-Help Techniques 6:
THOUGHTS AND BELIEFS

Depression is bound up with the way you think and what you believe. Although some people claim that depression is caused by negative or distorted thinking, this is far from clear. It is more likely that changes in your mood following negative and stressful life events change your beliefs and alter the way you think. Nevertheless, once this has happened, your negative and distorted thoughts cause your mood and energy levels to fall still further in a vicious downward spiral. This descent into depression can be interrupted by challenging and modifying:

o   The things you believe
o   The way you think
o   The actions you take in response to your thoughts and feelings.

You can be supported in modifying your thoughts, beliefs and behaviours by a Cognitive Behavioural Therapist – available via the NHS or Job Centre Plus. However, there can be long delays to access this support. And there are things you can do for yourself:

51. **Remember – half of everything you know is wrong... and you don't know which half**
52. **Thoughts are open to challenge**
53. **Be aware of distorted thinking**
54. **Be aware of how your thoughts make you feel**
55. **Be aware of how your thoughts and feelings make you behave**
56. **Learn to be kind to yourself**
57. **Avoid crystal ball gazing**
58. **Learn to be present**
59. **Learn to change negative thoughts into positive ones**
60. **Set positive, but achievable, goals**

51. Remember – half of everything you know is wrong… and you don't know which half !

People used to believe that the world was flat, the moon was made of green cheese, the sun would never set on the British Empire, there would be a Woolworths store on every high street, that mp3 threatened the music industry, etc. Beliefs and certainties are like that – at the time, we are sure they are true. But looking back it is clear that they weren't.

This is as true of our personal beliefs as it is of those held by society. It is particularly true of the kind of beliefs that you develop when you become depressed. You may believe "I am a failure" or "nothing good ever happens to me" or "I will never recover". But the evidence is against you.

So question your beliefs and the thoughts that flow from them. You might well find they are untrue.

52. Thoughts are open to challenge

Just as beliefs may not be true, so you do not have to take your thoughts at face value either. This is particularly true of the negative thoughts that accompany depression.

One way of challenge a thought is to look at the evidence. For example, your friend hasn't phoned you and you think "she doesn't want to speak to me". But do you have proof that this is true? It might be that your friend is preoccupied with a problem of her own, or she could be under pressure at work.

A good way of challenging negative thoughts about yourself is to ask whether you would say the same thing of a friend or a loved one. For example, you might forget to do something and think "I am useless". But if a friend forgot to do something, would you say "s/he is useless"? The chances are you would not – and if you wouldn't say it of them, you shouldn't say it of you!

53. Be aware of distorted thinking

While there is no evidence that depression begins with negative and unrealistic thinking, distorted thoughts are bound up with depression. People who become depressed experience similar distorted thoughts, which left unaddressed serve to make depression worse.

Unfortunately, when you are depressed, distorted thoughts can seem real and true unless you know what to look out for.

While the exact thoughts may differ, people with depression share several types of distorted thoughts:

12 Thought Distortions

Distorted thinking is a very common component of depression. It is both caused by and a cause of depression. As depression takes hold, so you become pessimistic and begin to look on the negative side of everything. This in turn causes you to become more depressed.

While you are depressed, you may be convinced that your negative thoughts are true and reasonable. However, looked at objectively, you will find they are unreasonable and unrealistic.

It can help to look at whether your thoughts are distorted by checking against this list of 12 common thought distortions:

1. *All or nothing thinking*—you see everything in black and white terms. For example, you receive a "B" grade in an exam, and count this as failure because only an "A" counts as success.

2. *Discounting positives*—when you are made aware of positive things about yourself or your situation, you dismiss them as being unimportant.

3. *Dwelling on the negative*—you give too much credence to negative things about yourself and your situation, and allow yourself to turn these over and over in your mind.

4. *Emotional reasoning*—you allow your thoughts to follow how you feel. For example, you don't feel like doing something so you put it off.

5. *Fortune telling*—you allow your depression to influence the way you view the future. For example, your friend offers to take you out for the day and you think, "I will just end up feeling tired and miserable".

6. *Labelling*—you identify yourself with shortcomings. For example, instead of thinking "I made a mistake", you think "I am an idiot".

7. *Magnification*—you blow negative aspects of yourself or your situation out of all proportion.

8. *Mind reading*—you assume people have a negative opinion of you when there is no evidence for this. For example, your manager ignores you when you come into the office and you assume you have done something wrong, even though there are many alternative explanations (e.g., she might be preoccupied with her work, or she might be thinking about problems at home).

9. *Minimalisation*—you trivialise positive things about yourself or your situation.

10. *Over-generalisation*—you let yourself believe that a single negative event is part of a run of negative life events or even part of a negative life story.

11. *Personalisation*—you blame yourself for things that were wholly or partly beyond your control. You blame others in a similar way.

12. *"Shoulding"* - you beat yourself up by using words like should, ought and must. For example, "I must tidy my house before I can go out" allows you to fail if you achieve this target. Contrast this with "I will try to do some housework before I go out".

Being able to identify distorted thoughts is the first step to overcoming them.

54. Be aware of how your thoughts make you feel

Once you identify your distorted, negative and unrealistic thoughts, you will find that they affect the way you feel. Since these thoughts are negative, it is likely that your feelings will be affected in a negative way too. For example, if you think "things will never improve", you are likely to feel sad, hopeless and helpless.

Your thoughts and feelings are linked, so you may find that sometimes a negative feeling gives rise to a negative thought. At other times, it will be the thought that gives rise to the feeling.

55. Be aware of how your thoughts and feelings make you behave

Both negative thoughts and negative feelings will cause you to act in particular ways. Often this will mean engaging in "quick-fix" behaviours such as:

o   Drinking alcohol
o   Smoking
o   Using caffeine
o   Comfort eating
o   Social withdrawal
o   Casual sex.

This is a far from complete list. Quick-fixes can be any behaviour that makes you feel good in the short term, but which make things worse later on.

The important thing is to be aware of why you are engaging in particular behaviours. Is it because your thoughts and feelings are negative? If so, you are "quick-fixing".

56. Learn to be kind to yourself

The quick-fix behaviours that accompany depression are as much a way of beating yourself up as are the distorted thoughts and negative feelings that go with your depression. Unfortunately, thoughts, feelings and behaviours are difficult to change. If you smoke, for example, simply being told it isn't good for you is unlikely to make you give up.

The simplest way of overcoming the quick-fix behaviours that accompany depression is to substitute a healthy alternative. For example, instead of going to bed when you feel sad during the day, go for a walk, a jog or a bicycle ride. Instead of comfort eating, learn to prepare healthy meals.

Only you can decide what health promoting alternatives you engage in, as it is essential that you enjoy them. Nevertheless, if you can engage in healthy activity, you will find your thoughts and feelings will become more positive as a result.

57. Avoid crystal ball gazing

Perhaps the biggest barrier to recovery for people with depression is that we think we can predict the future. If you are depressed, your depression frames your view of everything – including the future. So you project negativity forward. This results in beliefs such as:

o "Things will never improve"
o "I will never get a job"
o "I will never find love".

Although these "predictions" are unfounded and unreliable, they can become self-fulfilling if you start to act on them. If you don't believe you will ever find love, you will give up looking!
Remember that none of us knows what the future holds, so challenge any thoughts you have about the future.

58. Learn to be present

By monitoring your mood, you will probably find that your depression (and the anxiety that often accompanies it) exists in the past and the future. That is, you are probably depressed about things that have happened in the past (even if it is the recent past), but are spending the present ruminating over what happened. Often this rumination will involve projecting negative events from the past into the future. This will give rise to thoughts and feelings of hopelessness and helplessness.

If you can get passed your tendency to worry, you may well find that the present is okay. If you can learn to relax, let go of thoughts and feelings, and let the future take care of its self, you may find that your perception of the present widens.

Learning some relaxation techniques can help you to bring yourself into the present.

59. Learn to change negative thoughts into positive ones

Once you are aware of the way your thoughts, feelings and actions interact, you can convert negative thoughts into more positive and realistic thoughts. This does not mean "looking on the bright side" or "pulling yourself together". Rather, it is about learning to structure your thinking in a way that is more likely to help you take positive steps to recovery.

The hallmark of a positive thought is that it is:

o   Personal – "I"
o   Present – "I am"
o   Realistic – "I am sometimes"
o   Affirmative – "I am sometimes physically active".

So, if you think, "I am unemployable", this will become a self-fulfilling prophesy. You will stop looking for work, and begin to sound and act in ways that will count against you in the eyes of potential employers. If, in contrast, you think, "I have transferable skills that I can use to find work", you are much more likely to take positive steps forward, such as finding out what demand there is for your skills or seeking training to bring your skills up to date.

60. Set positive, but achievable, goals

Changing the way your depression makes you behave, feel and think is an essential step to recovery. You will most probably need to change your circumstances too. This is where many of us fall down because we try to run before we can walk. We forget that depression is debilitating, and that (at least to begin with) we lack the energy to jump back into normal patterns of daily life.

If you are unemployed, simply saying "I will get a job" does not mean that you will. Even if you do everything by the book, there is no guarantee that the job will be yours. Similarly, if your relationship broke down, simply saying, "I will find someone else" does not mean that you will.

The best any of us can do once we have decided what we want to achieve is to shorten the odds against failure. "I will get a job" is unlikely to be achievable because it is too vague a goal:

o   What job?
o   Where?
o   When?
o   How will you find it?

Breaking goals down into smaller, achievable steps is the best way of eventually achieving your goal. For example:

o   "I am meeting the job broker tomorrow morning to find out what demand there is for my skills"
o   "I look online and in the local paper every week to see if there are other jobs that I could do"

o "I have arranged a meeting with the careers office to find out about training opportunities in my area".

Importantly, achieving these smaller steps will make you feel more positive about yourself and your situation even if they do not immediately result in your main goal.

Tim Watkins

Self-Help Techniques 7:
COPING WITH LOSS / MANAGING CHANGE

Most depression is triggered by unpleasant or stressful life events that involve either loss (eg, a death, ill-health, divorce/separation, redundancy) or change (eg, a new job, a change of manager, debt, having a baby). When you are depressed, it is tempting to ignore these events. However, tackling them is essential to recovering from depression.

Here are ten ways that you can cope with loss and manage change:

61. **Accept that change is inevitable**
62. **Loss and change is about more than bereavement**
63. **Learn about grieving and be aware of how loss affects you**
64. **Plan the practical things you have to do**
65. **It's okay to ask for help**
66. **Find positive ways to express your feelings**
67. **Be prepared to try new things**
68. **Be open to new opportunities**
69. **Re-adjustment will take as long as it takes**
70. **Remember the rest of your life starts today!**

61. Accept that change is inevitable

Although most of us prefer stability, life is a process of change. All of us grow old. We change jobs. We enter into and end relationships. Some develop poor health or become disabled. Some get into debt.

When you are depressed, it is tempting to chew over what might have been and simply regret the situation you have lost. While you should respect these feelings and thoughts, it is important not to get trapped in them. Accepting change is an important step in moving on.

62. **Loss is about more than bereavement**

The experience of bereavement is common, but because our society tends not to talk about death, you may be unsure if what you are feeling is "normal". Broadly, people go through 12 stages of bereavement (although you may not actually experience all of them, and some will pass quicker or slower than others)

- **Emotional numbness**—a kind of shock reaction that switches off psychological pain in the same way as shock switches off physical pain fallowing trauma.
- **Denial**—behaving as if (and sometimes believing) the situation has not changed and that the loss has not happened. This can lead to a false sense of recovery.
- **Yearning**—having a profound longing for the situation or person that you have lost.
- **Negotiation**—where you enter into an internal dialogue with your-self, God, or some other higher being in a vain attempt to bargain for the past situation to be restored.
- **Agitation, anger and a sense of injustice**— in which you develop anger and rage over why this has happened to you— Why me? Why this? Why now?
- **Helplessness and hopelessness**—the realisation that things can never go back to the way they were, and the fear that you will never be able to move on with your life.
- **Depression**—you develop symptoms of depression, such as disrupted sleep, profound sadness, exhaustion, impaired memory and concentra-tion. There is a concern that you might become depressed for a pro-longed period, and that this may prevent you moving on with your life.
- **Guilt**—both about things left over from the previous situation and about beginning to move on with your life.
- **Silence and withdrawal**—even as you move on with your life and begin to recover, you may have periods when you slip back into the grieving process. This is particularly true of

times when you are re-minded of how things used to be, such as Christmas, anniversaries and birthdays.

o **Tearfulness**—becoming overwhelmed by memories of the past situation when they arise.

o **Self-pity**—feeling sorry for yourself about the situation you were left in.

o **Acceptance, letting go, moving on**—where you incorporate the change/loss into your wider life experience and are able to let go of the previous situation and move on with your life.

The process of bereavement does not only apply to the death of a loved one. Other situations involving loss can involve a similar process. These might include: children leaving home; change or loss of a job; friends moving away; leaving school or college; divorce or separation; illness or disability; retirement.

63. Learn about grieving and be aware of how loss affects you

Each of us responds to life events in our own way. The way in which you experience grief will be different too. Thinking about how you respond to loss, and relating these to the grieving process will help you to identify your personal way of dealing with loss or change.

From this, you can begin to look at the things that you do that are helpful and unhelpful. For example, in the past, you might have responded to loss by comfort eating, but this may have lowered your mood because you put on weight. Being aware that you might be tempted to comfort eat will allow you to develop healthier alternatives such as eating healthier foods or engaging in physical activity.

64. Plan the practical things you have to do

Most processes of loss and change will have a practical dimension that cannot be ignored. For example:

- o Deaths have to be registered, and you will need to talk to an undertaker
- o If you have lost a job, you may need to claim benefits and contact your insurance company
- o If you are going through a separation or divorce, you may need to use mediation or get legal advice

When you are depressed or stressed and upset, these practicalities can be overwhelming, and it is easy to ignore them in the (unrealistic) hope that they will go away. This usually makes matters worse.

Planning can help you manage the practicalities in a manner that doesn't wear you out. A plan can be anything from a simple "to do list" through to a more formal action plan – this will depend on the complexity of the task.

65. It's okay to ask for help

Self-help does not mean doing it alone. When you are coming to terms with loss or trying to cope with change, it is important to identify and engage with the wide range of agencies that offer help.

66. Find positive ways to express your feelings

Depression is worsened where feelings are not dealt with, or where they are turned inward. In the face of change and loss, you may find your feelings translating into guilt and self-blame. For this reason, it is important to take positive steps to express your feelings. This could be as simple as talking to a friend, or you might try:

- o Keeping a diary
- o Using arts and crafts
- o Talking to a professional counsellor
- o Talking to other people in a similar situation.

67. Be prepared to try new things

You may well wish that things could go back to how they were. A part of this desire can be that you avoid doing anything new.

But it is only by embracing new things that you can move on. Simply trying a new hobby or joining a new social group can create opportunities for you to move your life forward. This does not mean that you should force yourself to do things that you did not like in the past. But it does mean being positive about things that you have not tried before.

68. Be open to new opportunities

We all get caught up in beliefs about how our lives "ought to be". In the face of loss or change, it is easy for our beliefs to become very rigid as we try to hang on to the situation as it used to be. This can result in getting stuck – longing for a situation that has gone, but unable to move on.

Being open to opportunities (whether at work, in relationships or in recreational activities) is a key step to moving on with life and recovering from depression.

69. Re-adjustment will take as long as it takes

There is no timetable for coping with loss and managing change. Each of us does it differently. But one of the ways in which depression is worsened is when we beat ourselves up because we "shouldn't feel this way anymore".

Remember that in our society, nobody teaches you how to deal with loss and change. You have to learn by yourself, step by step, how to move on with your life. This is bound to take time. Taking time is not a mark of failure or inadequacy – it just means that you are doing things in your own way.

70. Remember that the rest of your life starts now !

No matter how bad you feel, and no matter how bleak the future looks, you will recover.

It is essential, though, that you do not wait until you have recovered to start getting on with your life – that would be like a fat person waiting until they had lost weight before going on a diet, or an unfit person waiting until they are fit before taking up exercise – it is the wrong way round.

Find ways of expressing yourself, re-engaging socially, trying new activities and being open to opportunities can be done despite you being depressed. The more you do them, the more pleasant they will feel, and the less depressed you will become.

Self-Help: Bringing it together

Recovery, personal wellbeing and resilience to further episodes of depression involve bringing all of the elements of our being into line. Imagine one of those old combination locks that requires you to bring all of the wheels into line to unlock it. For optimal wellbeing we all need to align our:

o   Social being
o   Physical being
o   Emotional being
o   Mental being
o   Core skills and abilities.

When you have all of these elements working together, you will experience a sense of "flowing" or what top sportsmen and women refer to as "being in the zone" – everything you do seems to work easily and seamlessly.

Often, people feel drawn to one or other element of self-help. For example, one person might want to improve their diet while another will decide to be more physically active. It is important to follow through with any activity or lifestyle change that you feel drawn to.

Take small steps
Adopting a healthier lifestyle or taking up new activities can be daunting. It is all too easy to allow yourself to be put off. You must battle against the inertia and limitations that come with depression. It is all too easy to think that the task is not worth starting because you do not believe you will ever finish it. Moreover, at the start, your depression may lead you to feel exhausted and more unwell— particularly if you try to do too much too quickly.

The trick is to take everything in small manageable steps. This is rather like someone training to run a marathon. There is no point just arriving on the day. You have to train regularly for month after month, gradually building your endurance to get to the point where you can do it. With depression, you have to start where you are, not where you wish you could be. If, for example, prolonged social withdrawal has led to agoraphobia, there is no point expecting to go out shopping immediately. However, you might sit in the garden. And when you are comfortable with this, you might build up to walking along the street, then, perhaps, to using a local shop, etc. Taken gradually, you will get back to full social engagement. It is just a matter of time and patience.

Draw up a plan

Adopting a healthy diet might require some thought and planning. There is no point shopping for fresh ingredients if you have not first learned how to store, prepare and cook them.

The first step might be to learn to cook. This could be by getting a friend or relative to show you how it is done. It could involve learning from a book, DVD or internet site. It could involve attending an adult learning class.

Buying healthy ingredients needs to be thought about. Do you want the convenience of buying everything in one go? Or would they prefer to shop around. Can you afford to buy whatever you want? Or do you need to get value for money? This will determine whether you shop at a single supermarket or whether you visit a range of different outlets.

The danger with depression is that you will "do it tomorrow". But tomorrow never comes. Writing a plan can help you stay on track, and it can help you to keep motivated.

Remember to work at your own pace. If you are very poorly and cannot do much, something as simple as doing some things around the house can be planned. Indeed, done properly, this can help provide a sense of achievement. Saying, "I will clean the house" is unlikely to work. But setting out a plan allows the task to be broken into achievable chunks. For example:

Monday:

10.30—pick up clutter in the living room

11.00—put rubbish in the bin

12.00—vacuum the living room

14.00—pick up clothes from bedroom

14.30—load washing machine

These can be ticked off as they are achieved:

10.30—pick up clutter in the living room ✔

11.00—put rubbish in the bin ✔

12.00—vacuum the living room ✖

14.00—pick up clothes from bedroom ✔

14.30—load washing machine ✔

In this way, you can see the things you have done rather than focusing on the things you have not. Also, you can be more aware of any problems you may have had. For example (remembering that someone with mental health problems can quickly become tired) you may have been unable to do the vacuuming because you had overdone things earlier, and may have needed to rest. Knowing this means you can scale down the things you plan to do next time.

This process of planning and breaking activities down into small manageable chunks can be applied to anything you want to achieve.

Keep a diary

Along with any plans you make, it can help to keep a record of health-promoting activities that you engage in every day. Over time, this can help you understand how some things make you feel better and some things make you feel worse.

For example, you could check your mood and energy levels against things like:

o   The amount of sleep you are getting
o   The amount of physical activity you do
o   Your diet (based on 5-a-day)
o   Your fluid intake (6-glasses-a-day)
o   Your alcohol intake
o   Any other quick-fixes
o   Your daily achievements.

Someone looking back through their record may find that when they over-use alcohol on Friday and Saturday they go on to experience low mood and energy levels on Monday and Tuesday. Similarly, someone may try doing exercise on Monday and claim that it leaves them feeling tired. But checking the record may show that in weeks when they did exercise on a Monday, their mood and energy levels were much improved on Tuesday and Wednesday.

Endnote: Recovery and Self-help

Recovery from depression is a process rather than an event.

There is no day or week when the depression disappears. Rather, as recovery gets going, there are days that include more "good hours", then there are weeks that include more "good days", and months that include more "good weeks".

These "good times" are the times when your mood is up-beat, and your energy has increased. During these times, it is important to engage with the many things that promote recovery while avoiding those things that cause you to become depressed.

The self-help approaches set out in this book are by no means exhaustive – you may well be able to identify self-help techniques of your own. The important thing is that you take the time to put them into practice. Because, in the end, treatment can help, self-help books can help, advice and support can help, but only *you* can bring about recovery from *your* depression.

While the journey may look long and daunting, for all of us it begins with a single step.

About Life Surfing

Life Surfing is a Cardiff-based not-for-profit Community Interest Company that was established to provide a coaching, mentoring and training approach for people experiencing common life problems that can cause stress, anxiety and depression.

Our mission is to help people learn to cope with life without the need to call on over-stretched NHS services that are better deployed to help people with severe mental illness.

Over the years we have found that there is a huge amount that people can do to develop their personal resources and to foster their own wellbeing. In most cases, the real need is for encouragement, support, knowledge and skills.

This is what Life Surfing offers.

We have developed a range of services – one-to-one wellbeing coaching, training workshops, mentoring groups and a range of publications - to give you the knowledge, skills and motivation needed to address life's issues and overcome stress-related problems in a healthy way, and to promote your long-term personal wellbeing.

For further information, please visit the Life Surfing website:

www. life-surfing.com

info@life-surfing.com

Or you can contact us on: 0300 321 4514 / 07922 537 646

Life Surfing, Box 124, R&R Consulting Centre
41 St. Isan Road
Heath
Cardiff CF14 4LW